442 COSMIC & UNIVERSAL LAWS

by

Dottie Randazzo

442 Cosmic & Universal Laws

by

Dottie Randazzo

Creative Dreaming
P.O. Box 3258
Wilmington, DE 19804

All rights reserved. No part of this book may be reproduced or transmitted in any form or by any means, electronic or mechanical, including photocopying, recording or by any information storage and retrieval system, without permission from the author, except for the inclusion of brief quotations in a review.

Copyright 2012 © by Dottie Randazzo

ISBN 978-1-257-75940-8

Other Books by Dottie Randazzo

Praying 101 for Spiritual Enlightenment
Praying 101 for Men
Praying 101 for Women
Praying 101 for Kids & Teens
Praying 101 for Parents

The Feeling
Trust
Are you a Spiritual Hypochondriac?
Gardening at Night
When the Soul Cries
How to Escape an Abusive Relationship
How to Shit Money!

Fiction
The Blue Girl

442 Cosmic & Universal Laws
Dottie Randazzo

Introduction

Cosmic and Universal Laws may also be known as Cosmic and Universal Principals. Many believe that the word "law" means authority being placed on them. In this book "law" is a principle. The laws in this book are not federal laws, county laws or municipal laws.

During my research for this book, I found that many have conflicting opinions about whether a law is a cosmic law or a universal law. The following are definitions that I found on the world wide web.

442 Cosmic & Universal Laws
Dottie Randazzo

Cosmic Laws

Cosmic laws are the only things in life that never change. Cosmic laws do not break or bend. Cosmic laws are also known as God's order.

Universal Laws

Universal laws contain the knowledge that all living things, that all life has within it that vitality, that strength, to gather from itself all things necessary for its growth and its fruition.

How do we really know what a Cosmic Law is? How do we really know what a Universal Law is? How do we really know the difference between a Cosmic Law and a Universal Law? Is there really a difference? So many questions, yet so little information.

442 Cosmic & Universal Laws
Dottie Randazzo

Here are the definitions from dictionary.com:

Cosmic

> * Of or relating to the universe, especially as distinct from Earth.
>
> * Infinitely or inconceivably extended; vast.
>
> * Of or from or pertaining to or characteristic of the cosmos or universe; "cosmic laws"; "cosmic catastrophe"; "cosmic rays".
>
> *Inconceivably extended in space or time.

Universal

> * Of, relating to, extending to, or affecting the entire world or all within the world; worldwide.
>
> * Including, relating to, or affecting all members of the class or group under consideration.

442 Cosmic & Universal Laws
Dottie Randazzo

* Application or common to all purposes, conditions or situations.

* Of or relating to the universe or cosmos; cosmic.

* Knowledgeable about or constituting all or many subjects; comprehensively broad.

* Adapted or adjustable to many sizes or mechanical uses.

Laws

* The body of principles or precepts held to express the divine will especially as revealed in the Bible.

* A code of principles based on morality, conscience or nature.

* A way of life.

442 Cosmic & Universal Laws
Dottie Randazzo

* A statement describing a relationship observed to be invariable between or among phenomena for all cases in which the specified conditions are met.

This book is created with the intent of making you aware of the laws that exists, which are known as cosmic, universal or both. I have allowed you to make the cosmic/universal determination on your own.

The descriptions of these laws are brief and the reader is encouraged to seek further information on a law if more information is wanted. Some of these laws are so complex that an entire book could be written about just one.

Law of Abundance - The universe is continually producing, growing, expanding and thriving in an endless cycle of plenty. *See also Law of Opulence and Law of Success.*

Law of Acceptance – Give self-permission to receive abundance.

Law of Accountability – Any energy put out into the divine universe will return to the sender three times. You are responsible for your actions not just the results of those actions. You are accountable at the time the action is created.

Law of Action – No matter how one thinks or feels it is an action, which brings the thought, or feeling to manifestation.

442 Cosmic & Universal Laws
Dottie Randazzo

Law of Action & Re-action – For every action force, there is a corresponding reaction force, which is equal in magnitude and opposite in direction.

Law of Actuality – This is a law that exists in the mind but not necessarily in the material form. It does not have to have dimension. It does not have to have form. It is what is believed.

Law of Adaptation – Allowing and flowing easily within is the only constant thing in the universe.

Law of Adjustment – When the natural harmony of life is disturbed an adjustment must be made in order that the disrupted equilibrium may be restored. Also known as karma.

Law of Affection – Affection is a beam of love that may light upon a subject and create an object of adoration. This law holds closely but with open arms. This law possesses not, yet sacrifices nothing of itself, for it gives without an expectation, even from the joy of giving.

Law of Affinity – Like attracts like. Like waves or frequencies will attract like waves or frequencies. *See also Law of Attraction, Law of Pure Desire, Law of Paradoxical Intent, Law of Magnetism, Law of Coalesce, Law of Imaging, Law of Visualization and Law of Harmony.*

Law of Agreement – The foundational truths on which collaboration is based.

442 Cosmic & Universal Laws
Dottie Randazzo

Law of Akasha – A great cosmic law, which is the principal of the intelligence of substance.

Law of Alchemy – Every condition in life can be transmuted into glory and made divinely beautiful, no matter what the condition is. Also known as Law of Change & Transmutation.

Law of Alignment – Every physical body is energetically propelled through life along natural causes.

Law of All Destroying Angels – An aspect of the fundamental Law of Love. It concerns the psyche or soul and therefore its function is to further the spiritual interest of the true man and to demonstrate the power of the second aspect, the Christ Consciousness and the power of divinity. Also known as Law of Repulse.

Law of Allowance – Permits the unconditional allowance of one to experience life and all that it offers without judgment or interference in any way one chooses.

Law of Allowing – This is the principal of least action, of no resistance.

Law of Analogy – Know thyself. Allows for a being to arrive at an understanding of the God Force within him/herself and within the universe by understanding all aspects of his/her own being.

Law of Applied Effort – All things are amendable to hard work.

442 Cosmic & Universal Laws
Dottie Randazzo

Archetypal Law – This is a prototype for the echoing reflections of other laws and which serves as the skeleton or framework for other laws. The first Archetype Law is the Law of One; second, the Law of Two; third, the Law of Three. This apparent division is never-ending so long as the Law of Description is in effect.

Law of Ascension – Defines the high vibration frequency, which the soul of an incarnated being is resonating.

Law of Assimilation – Allows no particles to be built into our bodies that we, as spirits, have not overcome and made subject to ourselves.

Law of Association – This law is associated with the principle of sympathetic magic. Things react upon each other under certain imposed or imaginary conditions. *See also Law of Knowledge, Law of Names, Law of Contact or Contagion and Law of Similarity.*

Law of Assumption – The idea of believing what one says will come to past.

Law of Attention – What you give your attention to expands.

Law of Attraction – Ensures that all conditions and situations the soul desires for mastering material reality are drawn to the attention of the individual intellect by virtue of the oneness of universe energy. This law dictates that your thoughts, words and deed will attract similar thoughts; words and deed from those you have contact with. *See also Law of Pure*

Desire, Law of Paradoxical Intent, Law of Magnetism, Law of Coalesce, Law of Imaging, Law of Visualization, Law of Harmony and Law of Affinity.

Law of Attunement – Is a law of positive action and negative reaction.

Law of Authority – Whoever is liable, has the authority. The degree of liability dictates the degree of authority to be given.

Law of Averages – The outcome of random events will even out given a large enough sample. *See also Law of Probability and Law of Uncertainty.*

Law of Awareness – Until there is a being, which recognizes and acknowledges an existence, there is no possible way of conceiving that anything has been manifested or created.

Law of Balance – Is a statement for conserving personal energy and achieving the greatest proficiency. Each thought must be balanced by whoever creates it. *See also Law of Karma and Law of Justice.*

Law of Beauty – We can surround ourselves with physical, emotional and mental beauty. Beauty in any form gives us spiritual satisfaction and releases our inner potentials. Beauty is soul inspired. Ugliness is materialism inspired.

Law of Becoming – The essence of sattwa, birth, creating, causing, and emanation. *See also Law of Emanation.*

Law of Being – Is of a nature so incomprehensible to the finite mind of man that he can only sense it partially.

Law of Believing – What you believe, you receive. *See also Law of Prayer and Law of Petition.*

Law of Bivalence – Every proposition is either true or false. Possible objections are of two kinds.

Law of Bodhisattva – One who has transcended the need of earthly incarnations, but who has chosen to return to earth, to support others in achieving enlightenment is ruled by this law.

Law of Brotherhood – Law in which man thinks of his brothers and not of himself alone. *See also Law of Group Life.*

Law of Causality – Law of I (one) developed to action. All action is caused by entities.

Law of Causation – Works in harmony with the stars so that a being is born at a time when the positions of the bodies in the solar system will give the conditions necessary to experience his/her advancement in the school of life.

Law of Cause & Effect – To understand this law you must be aware that the universe is a sea of energy. For every action, there is equal and opposite reaction. For every effect, there is a cause. *See also Law of Compensation, Law of Creativity and Law of Threefold Return.*

Law of Ceaseless Motion – Which lies at the root of cosmic evolution, finds its reflection in both small and great; in the tiniest atom and in the most glorious sun; in the sentient life of the lowest organism, up to man, and from man onward through all the divine hierarchies to that sum total which is unnamable. *See also Law of Motion.*

Law of Challenge – Everything that is experienced is considered to be mystical – prophetic dreams, visions, clairvoyant, etc., must be challenged to see if it is a genuine psychic experience.

Law of Chance – Results when the Law of Magic is initiated without being in harmony with the Law of Unity. The Law of Gratitude is that law which does bring justice and balance for those actions, which occur under the Law of Chance.

442 Cosmic & Universal Laws
Dottie Randazzo

Law of Change – Change is ever and always present in all things and nothing remains static forever.

Law of Change & Transmutation – Every condition can be transmuted and everything is always changing. Also known as the Law of Alchemy.

Law of Changeability – Anything true is variable. The world has changed or transformed and will continue to change on the basis of this law. *See also Law of Variability.*

Law of Chaos – Chaos exists when the observing mind cannot accept what is. *See also Law of Order.*

Law of Choice – No matter what situation someone is in, they always have the power to choose. *See also Law of Free Will.*

442 Cosmic & Universal Laws
Dottie Randazzo

Law of Choice & Opportunity – Choices and opportunities present themselves moment-by-moment. Some choices hover around whether we choose or not, then they move on.

Law of Circle & Curve – Everything in the universe is now basically angular yet shifting into curve and progressing towards becoming the circle. When the circle is achieved total perfection will ensue.

Law of Circulation - All things in the universe are always flowing in circulation at an expanding rate.

Law of Coalesce – When you think on something it will attract like thoughts. *See also Law of Attraction, Law of Affinity, Law of Pure Desire, Law of Paradoxical Intent, Law of Magnetism, Law of Imaging, Law of Visualization and Law of Harmony.*

442 Cosmic & Universal Laws
Dottie Randazzo

Law of Co-Creation – Two working in co-creative action have the power of four working individually; and three working in co-creative activity have the power of nine; and four working in co-creative activity have the power of sixteen. And so on.

Law of Cognetics – A universal law of thinking. The current view of the situation can never be equal to the better view of the situation.

Law of Color – Colors are centers of attraction. Colors and light may be seen from afar, and they intrigue the consciousness. Color is healing and impacts the physical, emotional, mental and human body profoundly.

442 Cosmic & Universal Laws
Dottie Randazzo

Law of Coming Into Being – The baffling mystery present in the manifestation of life, which pervades every entity, great or small.

Law of Common Ground – When, two or more, individuals send healing or changing energy to a specific place. Usually used for problem solving.

Law of Compassion – Beings on the Upper Ladder of Life stoop down to lend a helping hand to their brothers on the lower rungs in order to enable them to mount the ladder.

Law of Compensation – The group of principles, which take into account our thoughts and actions in any incarnation from where a cosmic judgment is rendered according to the results of our thoughts and actions, our deeds and misdeeds - the principle of duality in action. Also known as karma. *See also Law of Cause & Effect and Law of Creativity.*

Law of Completion – One of the most satisfying feelings is the sense of having attained full closure on a project or lifetime. *See also Law of Dissolution and Law of Return.*

Law of Concealment – Most of the universe is unknown to us. It is also known as the unbridgeable gap between what people mean and what people say.

Law of Concentration – The act of focusing the mind on a given desire until ways and means for its realization have appeared. *See also Law of Cosmic Habit Force.*

442 Cosmic & Universal Laws
Dottie Randazzo

Law of Conformity – An individual is more likely to agree to proposals that are well received by the majority of other people in their group.

Law of Connection – Everything in the universe is connected.

Law of Consecration – Wherever one focuses one's mind with intense thought and with a certain intention or desire in mind one transmits energy to it. This law is a sub law of the Law of Evolution.

Law of Consequences – The principal of action and reaction.

Law of Conscientious Action – You should act in a manner that will ensure that you are behaving in accordance with what you would like to get back from the universe. Related to the Law of Karma.

Law of Consciousness – As your consciousness expands you create the space for opportunity and possibilities.

Law of Consciousness in the Material Plane – Consciousness cannot manifest as a unit in the material and therefore must lay aside the material body and enter the cosmic plane of consciousness.

Law of Conscious Thought – Conscious thought is responsible for everything that has been created.

Law of Consistency – When an individual announces, either verbally or in writing, that they are taking a position on an issue, then that person will strongly defend that position regardless of its validity or even in the face of overwhelming evidence against it.

Law of Constancy – Anything true is constant or eternal. *See also Law of Eternality.*

Law of Constant Renewal – The cycle of rebirth. *See also Law of Periodicity.*

Law of Contact or Contagion – Things which have once been in contact with each other continue to act on each other at a distance even after physical contact has been severed. This is the second sub law of the Law of Association, follows from the Law of Similarity.

442 Cosmic & Universal Laws
Dottie Randazzo

Law of Contagion – Things once in contact continue to interact at subtle levels after physical separation. *See also Law of Similarity.*

Law of Contiguity – The assumption that things once in contact (a part or while, for example) continue to affect each other even at a distance. *See also Law of Sympathy and Law of Similarity.*

Law of Continuity – Transitions occur through stages. These stages are a number of minute additions occurring in a moment of time.

Law of Continuity of Consciousness – The universe is a continuous and endless process of creation.

Law of Contraction – Activity will expand or contract to meet its imposed deadlines. *See also Law of Forced Efficiency.*

Law of Contradiction – No proposition can be both true and not true; or that nothing can be - without qualification - the case and not the case at the same time; or that nothing can - without qualification - both have and lack a given property at the same time. *See also Law of Identity, Law of Excluded Middle and Law of Non-Contradiction.*

Law of Contrast – When two items or people are different from each other, we tend to see them even more different if they are placed close together.

Law of Control – We feel positive about ourselves to the extent that we feel we are in control of our lives.

Law of Cooperation – We can step up to our responsibilities and do everything we can to help those who are working to expand the work of teaching.

Law of Correspondence – As it is above, likewise there is a corresponding action below. As it is within, likewise there is a corresponding action without. *See also Law of Equalities and Law of Essential Divinity.*

Law of Cosmic Habit Force – An intangible, unseen force, which is made tangible and visible in nature. When you fix your mind on repetitive thoughts it will take over and carry it to its logical conclusions. *See also Law of Concentration.*

442 Cosmic & Universal Laws
Dottie Randazzo

Law of Courage – Courage is the ability to not only face a danger but to risk an action to defuse that danger. Fear departs when action enters.

Law of Creation – All blessings are predicated. If you receive blessings from God, it is by obedience to this law. Also known as the Law of Production and the Law of Creation.

Law of Creativity – Every advance in human life begins with an idea in the mind of a single person. *See also Law of Cause & Effect, Law of Compensation and Law of Threefold Return.*

Law of Credibility – The ability of individuals to earn, receive and accept credit for what they do, and to refuse credit for anything they have not done.

Law of Currency Exchange – Energy flows like water or electricity in currents which may be tapped for use elsewhere, may be exchanged for other energies, or may be stored in containers like bottles, cups, etc. – to be used or exchanged at another time or place.

Law of Cycles – There are certain things best done in a certain cycle than another. Everything that has happened throughout the ages has happened in cycles. *See also Law of Rhythm.*

Law of Cyclical Return – You will continue to face obstacles until you learn how to overcome them. Also known as reincarnation.

Law of Death – The death of the ego and the awakening of one's consciousness. *See also Law of Sacrifice.*

Law of Decision – Every great leap forward springs from a clear decision to act. If we act boldly, unseen forces will come to our aid.

Law of Deliberate Creation – If we desire a thing and think of it often with positive emotion, and we believe we deserve that thing; we can achieve that thing much faster.

Law of Description – Serves as a tool for creative purposes. This law knows no morality. It is capable of creating anything for any individual. This relates to the Law of Magic in that anything described is on its course toward creating a manifestation to the degree of impact on its description. *See also Law of Suggestion.*

Law of Desire – Believing in your desire completely and never wavering in your thought creates that which you desire. *See also Law of Attraction and Law of Intention.*

Law of Detachment – In order to acquire anything in the physical universe, you have to relinquish your attachment to it.

Law of Dharma – The principal of "right action" this refers to that which is universally right, right for all who are affected by the action.

Law of Dichotomy – Allows effect to precede cause.

442 Cosmic & Universal Laws
Dottie Randazzo

Law of Differentiation – The differences in the world are part of the dynamic process whereby the universe is becoming conscious of its self and unfolding.

Law of Diminishing Intent – The time to act is when an idea is strong and an emotion is hot.

Law of Diminishing Returns – Something that is done over and over again loses its power.

Law of Discernment – Being totally in tune with what is the next step in your personal evolution. Also known as the Law of Differentiation.

Law of Discipline – Discipline is the surest means to greater freedom and independence. It provides the focus to achieve the skill level and depth of knowledge, which equates to more options in life.

442 Cosmic & Universal Laws
Dottie Randazzo

Law of Disintegration – The law that governs the destruction of the form in order that the indwelling life may shine forth in its fullness.

Law of Dissolution – Ashes to ashes, dust to dust. Everything that has a beginning has an end. *See also Law of Return and Law of Completion.*

Law of Distraction – Similar to the Law of Attraction, you focus your energy away from what you don't want in the direction of what you do want.

Law of Divine Affirmation – The power of thought and words, which affirm that you are what you believe yourself or your reality to be. As you think, so shall you be.

442 Cosmic & Universal Laws
Dottie Randazzo

Law of Divine Circulation – Whatever resources, energies, abilities and time one possesses must be used to promote the welfare of all beings. By circulating one's energies, we have it returned to us manifold.

Law of Divine Flow – By living in the moment and centering ourselves we flow from our higher self.

Law of Divine Invocation – This law applies to those working in service to others. It allows the ascended realms to move from the confines of the Law of Non-Intervention to act on our behalf. Also known as the Law of Right to Decree.

Law of Divine Love – Also known as "unconditional love" and is present at the molecular level in the heart of everything.

Law of Divine Manifestation – Requires the manifestor to believe that whatever is needed for one's growth and fruition, will be supplied by the universe, for whatever price the manifestor truly believes is fair.

Law of Divine Oneness – We live in a world where everything is connected to everything else.

Law of Divine Order – Everything is as it should be. There are no accidents. Your energy, translated into thoughts, words, emotions and deeds causes all your experiences.

Law of Divine Proclamation – The ability of an individual to express, speak or proclaim on behalf of the Divine Force is in direct proportion to the ability of the individual to cease expression, speech or proclamation on behalf of self.

Law of Drama – Expressed as the struggle that comes from the action (right or wrong) on the way to the result. *See also Law of Karma, Law of Cause & Effect, Law of Dharma and Law of Right Action.*

Law of Duality – Any concept or force may be divided into two totally opposite concepts or forces, each of which contains the essence of the other. *See also Law of Opposites, Law of Synthesis and Law of Polarity.*

Law of Duration & Density – The longer and more intense you focus on something, the more substance you have in that new visualization.

Law of Effectiveness – Effectiveness is the measure of truth. Whatever works and is effective is of worth and is universal – application by all beings regardless of race, religion or sex, etc. Any system, which creates results, may be adopted for one's benefit so long as the Law of Harmlessness is taken into account.

Law of Elevation – Refers to the ability of an individual to uplift a group who can in turn benefit humanity as a whole. Also known as the Law of Group Progress.

Law of Emanation – Emerges from the complexities of natural processes. *See also Law of Becoming.*

Law of Emotion – While the mind is the engine for creating reality, its fuel is emotion energy. As the mind becomes focused on an objective, emotion is the energy that gets it there at a speed determined by its strength. Low intensity emotion brings slower and unrefined results, while high intensity emotion produces quicker and more definitive results.

Law of Energy – Everything is connected and shares the same source. Also known as the Law of Oneness.

Law of Energy Conservation – In nature nothing is wasted. Nothing is destroyed. Things transform in a continuous flux.

Law of Enthusiasm – This law functions like a boomerang, bringing back to us that which we project onto others, either for good or ill.

Law of Entropy – Everything in the physical universe is born, grows to maturity and then breaks down.

Law of Equalities – The major linking agent in the universe is the energy of love. Our judgments attract judgments to us of equal measure. Spirit does not judge us, only humans do. Also known as the Law of No Judgments. *See also Law of Correspondence and Law of Essential Divinity.*

Law of Equipoise – The fair exchange of balance that creates stability for third dimension manifestation.

Law of Essence – The inability to-exist-by-itself of a non-independent part.

442 Cosmic & Universal Laws
Dottie Randazzo

Law of Essential Divinity – There is a universal energy or life force, which is the essence of all things. *See also Law of Equalities and Law of Correspondence.*

Law of Essential Unity – Every individual lives its life in the field sphere of a greater being. The greater being maintains the sphere for the lesser.

Law of Eternality – Anything true is constant. *See also Law of Constancy.*

Law of Eternal Unfulfillment – There never can be completion or fulfillment in any moment. For if there were, there would be no further movement, as each moment contains within itself all that is essential for that moment, so also each moment contains within itself an emptiness, an unfulfillment that is essential and necessary to lead to the next moment.

Law of Etheric Union – By contemplating a beloved person, you can create a psychic connection and strengthen your connection - even to the point of union. Also known as the Law of the Lower Four.

Law of Evolution – A progressive evolutionary march of body, mind and spirit. *See also Law of Consecration.*

Law of Evolution & Rebirth – A slow process of development carried on with unwavering persistence through repeated embodiment in forms of increasing efficiency whereby all are, in time, brought to a height of spiritual splendor in recognition of source and true identity. *See also Law of Periodicity.*

442 Cosmic & Universal Laws
Dottie Randazzo

Law of Example – Any person, concept or thing that is placed in a position of significance, may serve as an example for others to follow.

Law of Exchange – All living organisms survive through exchange with their surrounding environment.

Law of Excluded Middle – Every proposition is either true or not true. *See also Law of Identity, Law of Contradiction and Law of Non-Contradiction.*

Law of Exclusion – When anything is specifically mentioned to be done then everything else is excluded.

Law of Expanding Influence – Energy expands in the world and has influence in your personal arena and in the world at large. This law is a sub law of Law of Attraction.

Law of Expansion – A gradual evolutionary expansion of the consciousness in every form.

Law of Expansion or Inclusion – The expansion is the inclusion which results when the definition and description of a part or situation is expanded to include something else.

Law of Expectancy – When a person whom you respect expects you to produce a certain result, then you will tend to work towards fulfilling that expectation, whether the end result is positive or negative.

442 Cosmic & Universal Laws
Dottie Randazzo

Law of Expectation – Energy follows thought. What one expects or believes creates their experience. *See also Law of Fixation.*

Law of Expediency – One always tries to get the things wanted as quickly and as easily as possible with minimum regard to secondary consequences.

Law of Faith – When the principles of faith are applied it will produce victory in your life every time, all of the time, no matter what.

Law of Few – There are a few people in this world, which are gifted, to make certain ideas tip.

Law of Finite Senses – One's senses are finite. They are limited to the amount of information, which one can absorb and process at any given time.

Law of Fixation – Whatever one focuses his attention on he will create. *See also Law of Expectation.*

Law of Flexibility – Involves accepting the present moment for what it is whether good or bad.

Law of Force – Energy manifest itself in three forms, creative, transmissive and attractive.

Law of Forced Efficiency – There is never enough time to do everything, but there is always enough time to do the most important thing. *See also Law of Contraction.*

Law of Forgiveness – When you forgive you release anger and allow the Law of Grace to occur.

442 Cosmic & Universal Laws
Dottie Randazzo

Law of Freedom – Freedom is not a final state of being, but an ever expanding action of giving each other the space to create spaces for others, to create more spaces for still others yet to come.

Law of Free Will – Divine will grants each entity the right to direct and pursue his or her life and the quality of that life as it was presented, so long as he or she does not violate this same right of others. *See also Law of Choices.*

Law of Friends – When someone you trust or like asks you to do something, you are strongly motivated to fulfill that request.

Law of Fulfillment – All blessings are predicated. If you receive blessings from God, it is by obedience to this law. Also known as the Law of Production and the Law of Creation.

Law of Gender – Male and female are necessary for procreation. Like seeds, everything has a gestation, or incubation period.

Law of Generation – All the cells of life divide and reproduce. *See also Law of Split & Divide.*

Law of Giving – The opposite energy flow of receiving. Both energies work together. *See also Law of Receiving.*

Law of Giving & Receiving – If you wish to receive anything in your life, you first need to give it. Giving is the other side of receiving.

442 Cosmic & Universal Laws
Dottie Randazzo

Law of Godlikeness – Divine presence and power indwells all individuals in the form of the spirit born soul. This law calls for the integration of a survival dominated intellect with the universal wisdom of the soul.

Law of Good Will – The consciousness of sending thoughts of willing good to others.

Law of Grace – Anyone can apply the Law of Mercy to grant a pardon to one who has made a mistake, so that the karma may be set aside. *See also Law of Synchronicity.*

Law of Gratitude – A sense of satisfaction in knowing that energy, which has been given, receives its certain reward according to its nature. Energy that is given moves out on that curved and unequal line, and when extended far enough, can only return to its source bearing its appropriate gifts. *See also Law of Chance, Law of Magic, Law of Resonance and Law of Unity.*

Law of Gravitation – Newton's law: Each object in the universe attracts each other body. Also known as attraction and repulsion. *See also Law of Gravity.*

Law of Gravity – Things which are in harmony, gravitate together.

Law of Group Consciousness – An individual has the power to transform his reality; a group of individuals possess the power to create group consciousness, which is in proportion to the strength of focused attention united with intention.

Law of Group Endeavor – Energy is multiplied when a group of like-minded individuals get together and focus on the same intent.

Law of Group Life – Man should not think only of himself but of humanity as a whole. Also known as the Law of Brotherhood.

Law of Group Progress – Refers to the ability of an individual to uplift a group who can in turn benefit humanity as a whole. Also known as the Law of Brotherhood.

Law of Growth – A universal law of complexity growth that operates at a deep level of reality.

Law of Guidance – In the soul's journey, into the destiny of the human experience, this law allows it to reach its goal of creating heaven on earth. This law makes feasible peace and goodwill on earth.

Law of Habit – Virtually all that we do is automatic and the result of habit.

Law of Happiness – It is not who you are, what you do or what you have that determines happiness but how you feel about who you are, what you do and what you have.

Law of Harmlessness – The higher the being, the greater its expression of harmlessness. The wisdom aspect of the soul must also direct harmlessness as a result of love and compassion or else it may end up violating the Law of Self-Preservation.

Law of Harmonics – The vibrational nature of objects that governs the relationships between fundamental frequencies.

Law of Harmony – This is about not judging people. Create loving relationships with everyone and everything you come into contact with and the universe will pay you back in kind. All things in moderation. Be balanced in your time; honor yourself as well as others. This is a law within the Law of Attraction. *See also Law of Pure Desire, Law of Magnetism, Law of Coalesce, Law of Imaging, Law of Visualization, Law of Affinity and Law of Paradoxical Intent.*

Law of Harmony & Agreement – Efforts to manipulate, trick, coerce, or force another to behave in harmony and agreement will only disrupt previously established areas of harmony and agreement.

442 Cosmic & Universal Laws
Dottie Randazzo

Law of Harmonies – Everything in the universe is in unceasing action.

Law of Healing – Concerns the ability of one to channel energy from the source called God.

Law of Heredity – Like the seed so is the harvest.

Law of Higher Will – This is when we surrender our smaller self and will to the guidance of a higher will for the highest of all good.

Law of Honesty – Honesty sees things as they are, without an attempt to alter that, which is seen, either for purposes of advantage or out of fear.

Law of Identity – Everything is what it is and not another thing. *See also Law of Contradiction, Law of Excluded Middle and Law of Non-Contradiction.*

Law of Imaging – The process by which the Law of Attraction is set into motion. *See also Law of Attraction, Law of Affinity, Law of Pure Desire, Law of Paradoxical Intent, Law of Magnetism, Law of Coalesce, Law of Harmony and Law of Visualization.*

Law of Immortality – The cosmic is eternal and immortal. That which contains the essence of the cosmic in its inner core is likewise eternal and immortal, although, its outward form, vehicle or expression is subjected to change.

Law of Impermanence of All Things – All phenomena that appear in this world are nothing existing in a fixed form. Therefore, all phenomena of this world are always changing.

Law of Inclusion & Exclusion – When God announces what he desires man to do; God's decision eliminates all other approaches (i.e. Noah).

Law of Increase – As you sow so shall you reap. Like begets like.

Law of Increase of Life – Whatever you are grateful for, you are sure to receive more of it.

Law of Individuality – An individual "owns" oneself, and may do to or for oneself, what one chooses, so long as it does not infringe on the equal rights of others.

442 Cosmic & Universal Laws
Dottie Randazzo

Law of Inertia – It is easier for something in motion to stay in motion, conversely, once an object (or a person) is at rest, it is easier to stay at rest. *See also Law of Paradox, Law of Cause & Effect, Law of Microcosm & Macrocosm and Law of Vibration.*

Law of Infinite Data – There is always new information for one to learn.

Law of Infinite Universes – Each person sees his universe or world a different way. There are two other sub laws under this law, Law of Pragmatism and Law of True Falsehoods.

Law of Infinity – Is an expression of two gifts, free will and existence. We exist, creation exists and we always have choice.

Law of Information – All information is energy and carries energy and all energy is information and carries information.

Law of Intelligence – Any energy pattern of sufficient complexity will act intelligently when treated as an entity. The more complex an energy structure, the more intelligence it possesses.

Law of Intention – Energy must follow intention for that which is perceived as good to happen.

Law of Intention & Desire – There is always an infinite amount of energy and information present to create whatever you desire.

Law of Interfaces – Power exists in the interfaces of things. These are the "between" places that are not entirely one thing or another. Traditionally, these places include caves, grottos, towers, mountains, beaches, wells, crossroads and cliffs.

Law of Intuition – When we no longer depend upon the opinions of others for our self-worth then we can get in touch with our own source of intuition and wisdom.

Law of Inverse Proportions (Longevity) – The span of life is related to the rate of breathing.

Law of Inverse Transformation – Is to pray believing that you already possess what you pray for. *See also Law of Reversibility.*

Law of Joy – When individuals experience joy, happiness and inner peace, creation is observed dissolving the higher and lower selves, changing all into nameless fragments of the divine.

Law of Justice – Like scales of balance, that which is heavy on one side, must be balanced by that which is equally heavy on the other side. When one violates another, the heaver the violation the heavier must be the balancing weight. This is related to the Law of Karma and the Law of Balance.

Law of Karma – For every event that occurs, there will follow another event whose existence was caused by the first, and this second event will be pleasant or unpleasant according as its cause was skillful or unskillful. *See also Law of Balance and Law of Justice.*

442 Cosmic & Universal Laws
Dottie Randazzo

Law of Knowledge – With understanding, comes control and power. The more a person knows about a person or phenomena the more control he has over it. This law is a specific sub law of self-knowledge or "knowing thyself." *See also Law of Association and Law of Names.*

Law of Labeling – When we label anything we exclude true information concerning it. Labeling does not define a thing nor explain its true nature. Labeling results in confusion.

Law of Least Effort – Nature's intelligence functions with effortless ease and abandoned carefreeness.

Law of Leverage – A small amount of energy exerted to change the course of events at a present time (at the right moment) can move mountains in the future.

442 Cosmic & Universal Laws
Dottie Randazzo

Law of Liability - One is held liable for the use or abuse of whatever rights one has, and one is held liable for using or neglecting those rights.

Law of Liberty – All beings are free to express their pristine, innate nature, so long as; it does not harm anyone or anything. Anyone or anything that interferes with that expression violates this law and will be karmically responsible.

Law of Life – A system of laws that all beings are subject to and which serve to foster life.

Law of Light – Light will always defeat darkness by revealing information not previously seen, and it's this force that empowers humans.

Law of Living Truth - A dynamic individual experience, forever unfolding, always growing, expanding, and being differently perceived by each intellect.

Law of Lotus – The flowering of self and includes knowledge, love and sacrifice.

Law of Love – Places the welfare, concern and feeling for others above self. The Law of Love is that close affinity with all forces that you associate with as being "good". The Law of Love is the force that denies a place for evil in the world.

Law of Love & Light – Applies to the initiate who has transcended the stage of self-consciousness. Also known as the Law of Schools.

442 Cosmic & Universal Laws
Dottie Randazzo

Law of Lower Four – By contemplating a beloved person, you can create a psychic connection and strengthen your connection - even to the point of union. Also known as the Law of Etheric Union.

Law of Macrocosm & Microcosm – The first Law of Infinity. This law indicates that the whole is equal, more or less, to the sum of its parts depending on the ordering of those parts. In everything that exists there is within it some part of the whole. The whole is the grouping together of each of its parts in a certain order.

Law of Magic – The law that creates change. Physical change comes about through the change of consciousness. Consciousness changes in response to anticipation. Anticipation results from imagery and preparation, fears and desires based on fallacies or facts. Preparation for change changes consciousness, which results in physical change. The Law of Magic is an extension of the Law of Unity. *See also Law of Chance, Law of Gratitude, Law of Unity and Law of Description.*

Law of Magical Accounting – Any rebalance of the natural forces is performed, as a karmic payment is due. *See also Law of Balance.*

Law of Magical Names – There is a connection created by shared structure, a certain resonance. One's true name is related to the vibrational value or the frequency of one's soul-self.

Law of Magnetic Affinities – By astrologically choosing the time and place of your birth, you determine the nature of the effect you will experience in your life.

Law of Magnetic Control – One of the seven laws of our solar system. Every thought we have creates a match that comes back to us like a boomerang.

Law of Magnetic Impulse – The result of an eventual union between a man or atom and a group, which produces harmonious relations. Also known as the Law of Polar Union.

Law of Magnetism – You can only attract the same kind of energy that you put out. This is a law within the Law of Attraction. *See also Law of Affinity, Law of Pure Desire, Law of Paradoxical Intent, Law of Coalesce, Law of Imaging, Law of Visualizing and Law of Harmony.*

Law of Manifestation – Consciousness is always a choice, it's a choice to bring your awareness to the present moment, the decision to see and prioritize that that is truly important, that which is genuinely honoring and the value enhancing in your life. This is a law within the Law of Attraction.

Law of Mantras – The state where nothing exists but the mantra. When man forgets he is chanting.

Law of Matter & Force – Their exists an infinite and unchangeable quantity of atoms, the base of all matter and the base of all energy, and these are in a state of constant vibratory motion, infinite in extent, unchangeable in quantity, the initial of cell forms of energy.

Law of Meditation – Defined as a current of unified thought. The continuum of mental effort, to assimilate the object of meditation, free from any other effort to assimilate other objects.

Law of Mental Equivalency – To achieve success in any area, we must have a clear image of that success in our mind and a mental picture of our idea of success, a vision.

Law of Mentalism – All is mind; the universe is mental. Whatever exists exists as a thought in the cosmic mind.

Law of Mentative – That which is constantly drawing toward us the things we desire and also drawing us toward them.

Law of Mercy – Allows one to forgive all error, to forgive equally those who err against you as you err against them. This is to be merciful. To be merciful is akin to the Law of Love. *See also Law of Grace.*

Law of Mind – As you believe, so it will be.

Law of Mind Over Matter – Mind is always dominant over matter, and that spirit is ever correlated with its own creations throughout the universal energy field, permeates all levels of consciousness, if not awareness, sooner or later.

Law of Minimum Effort – Nature's cleverness functions with easy effortlessness.

Law of Miracles – Is possible by anyone who realizes that the essence of creation is light.

442 Cosmic & Universal Laws
Dottie Randazzo

Law of Momentum – When you are down, the universe works to keep you down. When you are up, the universe works to keep you up.

Law of Monadic Return – Within limits, man is the controller of his destiny wielding forces and energies. The more he controls the larger his radius.

Law of Money – Money is but an artificially created symbol used as a substitute to store energies borrowed, earned, spent, owed, claimed and exchanged.

Law of Morality – This law guarantees that supreme virtues will ultimately prevail for heaven on earth.

Law of Motion – Everything demonstrates the action of this law, for nothing can remain isolated or static.

Continuous change exemplifies the Law of Ceaseless Motion.

Law of Motivation – Wherein the motivation is the means, the end may discover the Law of Gratitude returning more quickly to them with greater abundance, than the energy that has been given.

Law of Names – Knowing the true and complete name of a phenomena or entity gives you complete control over it. *See also Law of Knowledge, Law of Association and Law of Words of Power.*

Law of Necessity – That which is necessary to fulfill the requirements of nature. Nature will always fill it with the best possible replacement at hand.

Law of Neutralization – The raising of the ego above the vibrations of the unconscious plane of mental activity, so that a negative swing (mood swing) is not manifested in the consciousness, and therefore the individual is not affected.

Law of New Being – Lessens polarities and reconciles oppositions. The Law of New Being reconciles the "yes" and "no", right and wrong, good and evil, and brings the concepts of God and Satan together in harmonious resolution, integrated totally under the Law of One.

Law of Nirvana – The ability of an entity to complete their reincarnations and grow their soul with the vibrational speed that allows them to merge with God.

442 Cosmic & Universal Laws
Dottie Randazzo

Law of No Judgments – Our judgments attract judgments to us of equal measure. Spirit does not judge us, only humans do. Also known as the Law of Equalities.

Law of Non-Attachment – An individual can free himself from the confines of a karmically determined existence. Enlightenment is attainable through the realization that the ultimate nature of self is empty.

Law of Non-Contradiction – Non-instance in the same respect can be in two or more contradicting states. *See also Law of Contradiction, Law of Excluded Middle and Law of Identity.*

Law of Non-Intervention – Prevents physical beings and non-physical beings from interfering or correcting what they see as wrong or harmful.

Law of Non-Resistance – Whenever you resist some situation, you are giving more power to it. What you resist always persist.

Law of Nothingness – This quiet center (<u>any</u> quiet center is <u>the</u> quiet center) is the place of infinite potential.

Law of Now – Past, present and future are illusory phenomena conceived by the conscious mind.

Law of Numerology – All things depends upon numbers. All things are created by numbers and controlled by numbers. Cosmic waves, vibrations, cycles and radiations are measured in frequencies and numbers, which are nothing more than numerical energy patterns.

442 Cosmic & Universal Laws
Dottie Randazzo

Law of Obedience – The more one obeys or aligns oneself with the way of nature, cosmic laws and one's true will, the greater will be one's progress or evolution toward the light.

Law of Octave – Collects all the processes of the universe. Can be applied everywhere to every process of whatever scale. *See also Law of Seven and Law of Septenary.*

Law of One – All laws reside within this law. That all souls are cells of the body. There is no need for anyone to struggle or compete. With the Law of One you are at peace in the body of awareness. All is one.

Law of Oneness – Everything is connected and shares the same source. Also known as the Law of Energy.

Law of Opportunity – When you are unconditionally ready for something, it will make its appearance known.

Law of Opposites – The synthesis of two opposing or conflicting ideas or pieces of data will produce a new, third idea that will not be a compromise of the original two. *See also Law of Synthesis, Law of Polarity and Law of Duality.*

Law of Optimism – A positive mental attitude goes with success and happiness.

Law of Opulence – The mental law of success. Through this law people attract things, people and events into their lives. *See also Law of Abundance and Law of Success.*

442 Cosmic & Universal Laws
Dottie Randazzo

Law of Order – Exists when the observing mind can accept what is, regardless of the appearance of chaos. *See also Law of Chaos.*

Law of Order of Creation – Is that which comes as a thought or feeling, grows in the mental region and manifest in the material.

Law of Oscillation – All phenomena oscillates/vibrates to various frequencies.

Law of Our Being – There are times when you have to obey a call which is the highest of all, i.e. the voice of conscience even though such obedience may cost many a bitter tear, and even more, separation from friends, from family, from the state to which you may belong, from all that you have held as dear as life itself.

Law of Paradox – Recognizes the movement of energies in four dimensions simultaneously. This law combines the Law of Cause & Effect, the Law of Inertia, the Law of Microcosm & Macrocosm and the Law of Vibration.

Law of Paradoxical Intent – Requires trust, letting go and knowing that happiness will come to you. Be very clear about your intent and do not allow yourself to be distracted. This is a sub law within the Law of Attraction. *See also Law of Pure Desire, Law of Affinity, Law of Magnetism, Law of Coalesce, Law of Imaging, Law of Visualization and Law of Harmony.*

Law of Parallelism – All phenomena exist in parallel with each other and have correspondences between them.

Law of Patience – All things must have their time and their season whereby they may work their action to proper fruition.

Law of Patterns – Patterns are information. Information is energy. The more information you have the less energy you may need to expend depending upon the correctness of the information.

Law of Peace – Warns that any compromise with forces that divide instead of unify, that oppress instead of liberate, that harm instead of benefit, will lead inevitability to greater conflict.

Law of Penetration – Anything that is looked at with great attention by great quality of consciousness penetrates to the heart, and then emanates into all of consciousness.

Law of Perfection – Everything is perfect and in its divine state.

Law of Periodicity – This is set forth in the axiom that for every period of activity there is a consequent interval of rest, observable in nature as day and night, the flow and ebb of tides, the process of waking and sleeping, birth and death. One phase of this law that manifest is the Law of Constant Renewal, in which the necessity for rebirth, or reimbodiment, is demonstrated.

Law of Perpetual Increase – Be grateful for everything and you will constantly receive more of everything.

Law of Perpetual Motion – Everything exists with an opposite.

442 Cosmic & Universal Laws
Dottie Randazzo

Law of Perpetual Transmutation – Energy is forever changing and moving into physical form and back to pure energy again. Energy is in a constant state of transmission and transformation.

Law of Persistence – Our ability to persist, despite setbacks and disappointments, affirms our belief in ourselves.

Law of Personification – Any concept, force, object, or phenomena may be considered to be alive, to have a personality and /or to be an entity. Corollary to this law are the sub laws of invocation and evocation.

Law of Petition – Thought in the form of a solemn request, or prayer, influences energy and is "received" throughout the universe. *See also Law of Believing and Law of Prayer.*

442 Cosmic & Universal Laws
Dottie Randazzo

Law of Physical Evolution – As each atom changes by losing particles of itself by virtue of the law of change we note that these particles are gathered to form a new mass.

Law of Physical & Mental Evolution – No society could advance if every man was smaller than his place. This law guides social evolution.

Law of Planes of Correspondence – Enables one to operate on a higher plane of intuition and discernment.

Law of Planetary Affinity – The connection and interaction, which the planets have with each other.

Law of Polarity – Anything can be separated into two opposite parts with each part having its own essence.

See also Law of Opposites, Law of Synthesis and Law of Duality.

Law of Polar Union – The result of an eventual union, between man or atom and the group, which produces harmonious relations. Also known as the Law of Magnetic Impulse.

Law of Portrayal – Any action portrayed cultivates the attitude of that action to the degree and impact of the energy involved in that portrayal; and with repetition, can mold a real life character quality that emanates and expresses the qualities of that action, with all its accompanying feelings, behaviors and patterns of expression.

Law of Poverty – The degree to which one withholds one's productivity and energy in hopes someone else will offer theirs instead, an entity earns and experiences poverty proportionally.

Law of Power – Everything is energy, therefore everything has power, the power to influence, the power to create, to manifest, to sustain and to destroy.

Law of Pragmatism – If it works, it's true. *See also Law of Infinite Universes and Law of True Falsehoods.*

Law of Prayer – Whereby man and God each have a part to play. Man offers the prayer and God answers if he deems it worthy of being answered. *See also Law of Believing and Law of Petition.*

Law of Preparation – Perfect performance comes from painstaking preparation.

442 Cosmic & Universal Laws
Dottie Randazzo

Law of the Present Moment – When we practice remembering that the here and now is all we have our present moments improve.

Law of Preservation – God created all living things to live life to its fullest.

Law of Principal – This law gives humans the perception of basic rules of the cosmos. It ensures moral means to moral ends, a voluntary association in governing practices.

Law of Privacy – The divine law that every person is entitled to the sanctity of his or her own privacy.

Law of Probability – The more possibilities and options that you include, the lower the chances will be for a particular outcome to happen. *See also Law of Averages and Law of Uncertainty.*

Law of Process – A knowing to appreciate all steps in the accomplishment of a goal.

Law of Production – All blessings are predicated. If you receive blessings from God, it is by obedience to this law. Also known as the Law of Fulfillment and the Law of Creation.

Law of Progress – The energies at work when manifesting.

Law of Progression – Throughout space there is a constant change or progression.

442 Cosmic & Universal Laws
Dottie Randazzo

Law of Progression of Contraries – This world progresses by the interplay of contraries. Without contraries no progression exists.

Law of Projection – The film that projects, depicts and creates the events of one's life story is stored within one's consciousness and can only be changed from within.

Law of Promotion – Someone whose laws you have followed can only promote you.

Law of Prophecy – The only future that exists is of the desire and/or free will of all creation.

Law of Prosperity – One prospers in direct proportion to the enjoyment one receives in seeing the prosperity of oneself and others.

Law of Psychic Phenomena – There is a power within which can communicate without the tongue, hear without the ear, see without the eye, talk without the mouth, move objects and grasp things without the hand.

Law of Pure Desire – Requires that what you desire must be pure and motivated by love and passion. An element of ego cannot be present. An element of urgency or lack cannot exist. Total detachment and surrender must be exercised. This is a law within the Law of Attraction. *See also Law of Harmony, Law of Affinity, Law of Magnetism, Law of Coalesce, Law of Imaging, Law of Visualization and Law of Paradoxical Intent.*

Law of Pure Potentiality – Based on the fact that we in our essential state are pure consciousness.

442 Cosmic & Universal Laws
Dottie Randazzo

Law of Purity – We can purify our bodies, emotions and minds. Purity is a state in which the human soul is in full control of his mechanism and runs that mechanism in harmony with a plan and purpose of life.

Law of Purpose – Everyone has a purpose in life, a unique gift or special talent to give to others.

Law of Radiation – Every substance radiates energy to a lesser or a greater degree. Since nothing in the universe is ever still, energy in beings or substances is in a continuous motion and is in a compositional or a decompositional state. Radioactive substances represent energy in the state of dispersal.

Law of Reality – Is measured by empirical formulae, which are set up in relation to dimension. If an object can be seen, heard, measured, felt, then this object is said to have reality.

Law of Rebirth – All souls incarnate and reincarnate.

Law of Rebound – A superior force will always rebound a lesser force.

Law of Recapitulation – We are born innocent and gain experience in life to die and be reborn innocent only bring back what is essential to us.

Law of Receiving – The opposite energy flow of giving. Both energies work together. *See also Law of Giving.*

Law of Reciprocity – To give and take mutually, to return in kind or even in another kind or degree.

Law of Recognition – Everything you need in your life is already in your life merely waiting your recognition of it. Anything unrecognized becomes uncelebrated. Anything uncelebrated becomes unrewarded. Anything unrewarded eventually exits your life.

Law of Reconciliation – That which finds, in differing qualities, unifying similarities that allow these differences to be brought together to accept the unifying qualities and diminish the differences. So the differences in qualities become less clashing and conflicting whereby the unifying qualities become more binding.

Law of Records – Every event that occurs in the universe is not lost. They are indelibly imprinted upon the Akashic Records also known as the "Book of Records".

Law of Re-Embodiment – Man reincarnates under the demands of karmic liability, under the pull of that which he as a soul has initiated and because of a sensed need to fulfill instituted obligations. He also incarnates from a sense of responsibility to meet requirements, which an earlier breaking of the laws, which govern right human relations, have imposed upon him.

Law of Reflection – The use of a name repetitively is linked to the person or object it represents.

Law of Regeneration – Regulates reproduction in nature. The same species reproduce the same species.

Law of Reincarnation – Each individual is granted the right and chance to experience everything at their own rate and selected method. This is to ensure that each individual gets all the pieces needed to complete the cycle necessary for fulfillment.

Law of Relationship – All parts or partners are in relationship, though some are close and some are remote.

Law of Relativity – The relationship of all things understood by the particular viewpoint from which they are seen. As the viewpoint shifts the perceived relationship of those things also changes.

Law of Relative Truth – There are two kinds of truth in the cosmos, one absolute, the other relative. The absolute truth is unchanging and eternal. Relative truth has many facets and is ever changing. It is illusory in one sense and in another real only to those who have conscious awareness of it or give it credence.

Law of Reproduction – You can only reproduce something you are.

Law of Repulse – An aspect of the fundamental Law of Love. It concerns the psyche or soul and therefore its function is to further the spiritual interest of the true man and to demonstrate the power of the second aspect, the Christ Consciousness and the power of divinity. Also known as the Law of All Destroying Angels.

Law of Repulsion – This is working in reverse of the Law of Attraction. In this law one may say, the point of attraction is now space itself – this results in disintegration.

Law of Resistance – That which you resist you draw to you.

Law of Resonance – Like energies attract like particles due to their electromagnetic fields. Thoughts, words or actions are amplified and return to us. *See also Law of Gratitude, Law of Chance, Law of Magic and Law of Unity.*

Law of Respect – The principal of looking twice or more precisely looking twice as deeply. Respect goes beyond the surface appearance and superficial glances to discover a deeper meaning, purpose or basis for discovery. *See also Law of Tolerance.*

Law of Responsibility – One entity or more working in a manner that is responsive to the needs of many receive energy from those many.

Law of Resurrection – Aids all life units to transcend limitations and barriers and ascend into higher states of consciousness, more expanded horizons, more glorious vehicles and relationships with divine beings. This law provides us with cosmic dispensations, techniques and principles that when taken advantage of results in rapid soul advancement.

Law of Retribution – Even if you have done no wrong in this life, you could still be suffering owing to past karma (good and bad deeds) of previous life/lives.

Law of Return – Going home. Yearning to return to the beginning. *See also Law of Dissolution and Law of Completion.*

Law of Revelation – A breakthrough in your perception where you flash on the deep meaning of a word or an event. An *'aha'* experience.

Law of Reverse Effort – The harder you try, the more the process becomes a tedious chore to be endured.

Law of Reversibility – Because all transformations of force are reversible, one should always assume the feeling of their fulfilled wish. This law enables one to foresee the inverse transformation once the direct transformation is verified. *See also Law of Inverse Transformation.*

Law of Rhythm – Everything moves in perfect rhythm and at perfect speed. *See also Law of Cycles.*

Law of Ricorsi – (1) To recur, to return; upon the start of itself; to be cyclical. (2) Ricorsi is the pure form of reflection, the turning or bending back of mind upon itself. Also known as Vico's Law.

Law of Right Action – Your energy is self-perpetuating in the world. Value, honor and dignity will increase in your life to the same degree that you promote them in the environment around you. This is a law within the Law of Attraction.

Law of Right Human Relations – This law helps us find control with others in the third dimension. It states, "Let no one assume to forcibly teach, counsel or guide, for we all have the greatest we can hope for within us".

Law of Right to Decree – This law applies to those working in service to others. It allows the ascended realms to move from the confines of the Law of Non-Intervention to act on our behalf. Also known as the Law of Divine Invocation.

Law of Right to One's Own Space – Everyone is entitled to make decisions for their self. Decide a belief system, which they feel comfortable with, and create the life that will allow them to fulfill his/her birth vision.

442 Cosmic & Universal Laws
Dottie Randazzo

Law of Scarcity – When a person perceives that something or someone they want is in limited quantity. The perceived value of that which they desire is greater than if it were overly abundant.

Law of Sacrifice – States that you have to give up something to get something. Also known as the Law of Those Who Choose to Die. *See also Law of Death.*

Law of Schools – The evolutionary progress of a spiritual person. This law comes into effect as the human consciousness expands to a certain degree. With the expansion comes the attraction of teachers. Also known as the Law of Love and Light.

Law of Security – Provides a foundation upon which an entity stands whereby the entity can select a form of expression that allows his or her best performance without infringing on the security or expression of others who have the same rights.

Law of Seed – What you have in your hand will create anything you want in your future.

Law of Self-Knowledge – One who does not know himself, having never tested himself or his limitations does not know what he can do. This is the sub law of the Law of Knowledge.

Law of Self-Preservation – Every life unit is striving to maintain and sustain its existence at some level and attempting to exist on a higher spiral of being, a higher life expression. Going contrary to this law, as in suicide, where the desire is to terminate self-existence is a crime against nature.

442 Cosmic & Universal Laws
Dottie Randazzo

Law of Self-Unfoldment – This is demonstrated by the urge that causes every entity to seek to express itself in accordance with its essential characteristics.

Septenary Law – The prevalence of the number seven. Seen in the 7 days of the week, 7 colors of the rainbow, 7 notes on the musical scale, 7 planes, 7 Lokas & Talas, 7 Tattvas or element principals, 7 cosmic principals and the sevenfold constitutions of man. Also Law of Seven. *See also Law of Octave.*

Law of Service – Our rewards in this life will be in direct proportion to the value of our service to others.

Law of Seven – The prevalence of the number seven is seen in the 7 days of the week, 7 colors of the rainbow, 7 notes on the musical scale, 7 planes, 7 Lokas & Talas, 7 Tattvas or element principals, the 7 cosmic principals and the sevenfold constitutions of man. Also known as Septenary Law. *See also Law of Octave.*

Law of Sex – All things shall balance themselves out if left to the force of universal law as guided and unhampered by a mind of conscious control. Also applies to the attraction between the sexes.

Law of Silence – Allows entities the space, peace and time to rest and recuperate from the noises and chattering outside. This silence is found within the soul and is not limited to sound but also relates to forms of motion, emotion and feelings.

Law of Similarity – Like things produce like things. An effect resembles its cause. This is the first of two sub laws contained within the Law of Association; the second is the Law of Contact or Contagion.

Law of Solar Evolution – The sum total of all the lesser activities.

Law of Solar Union – When the interplay of the suns is being dealt with from the material aspect and from the consciousness aspect. This term is used occultly.

Law of Soul Evolution – Soul evolution is the goal of everyone on earth. We reincarnated to evolve spiritually.

Law of Soul Mind – Soul is of a nature so incomprehensible to the finite mind of man that he can only sense it partially. The soul mind knows of the natural subtle cosmic laws of the universe and the oneness of all things, as well as, the great diversity of creation.

Law of Soul Rights – Constantly at work on behalf of the soul; to be self-governing in the physical body.

Law of Sound – Every living thing in existence has a sound.

Law of Sowing & Reaping – For those who refuse to give up and continue to do things right, for those who are persistent and do not get discouraged even when nothing happens rewards will follow.

Law of Spirit – Spirit is the only way to accomplish prefect unity and harmony that will abolish governments, religious belief systems, jails, the military, courts, religious leaders, etc.

Law of Spiritual Approach – Depicts the conscious act of a personality to create with its every thought, word and deed the ability to be the reflection of its god self.

Law of Spiritual Awakening – A basic level of self-control and stability is needed to maintain the degree of effort required for the awakening of other states of awareness.

Law of Split & Divide – This is the law of generation. All plant, animal, human life, as well as, the life of the corporate business, splits, divides and diversifies in the process of branching out. This law normally functions automatically in nature. At some levels man may personally direct this law.

442 Cosmic & Universal Laws
Dottie Randazzo

Law of Striving Toward Profection – It is striving that balances our knowledge and our beingness. The future of humanity will be determined by our striving toward higher ways of life.

Law of Subconscious Activity – Our subconscious mind alerts us to things around us that are consistent with our dominant desires and concerns.

Law of Subconscious Mind – One is not able to distinguish fact from fiction. If it is convinced a false statement is true, it will act as if one were true.

Law of Subjective Value – All value is in the eyes of the beholder.

Law of Submission – Where one simply allows the higher intelligence to do its work through our consciousness without any ego interference and without mapping out the results or outcome. The Law of Sacrifice is related to this law.

Law of Substance – Existence is described like an onion wherein one layer of description is surrounded by another layer of description, encased within another layer of description and so on.

Law of Substitution – A part may signify the whole, a genus may be signified by a species, and a cause may be signified by an effect or vice-versa. There can be any item substituted for the concept or any concept substituted for the item. The substituted article, concept or event can affect that which it was substituted for.

Law of Success – Governs how and what we create. *See also Law of Abundance and Law of Opulence.*

Law of Sufficiency & Abundance – You have everything within you right now to make your life a living dream.

Law of Suggestion – A statement carries with it an impact. Associated with the Law of Description.

Law of Summons – One can learn to lift the soul from the physical body and summon another soul to have a soul-to-soul talk.

Law of Supply & Demand – This is the applied will and word spoken with emotion, which does supply any man that which he demands if it is done in a correct manner. It is commonly applied in a slightly difference sense in the field of business and economics.

Law of Surrender – When we stop resisting the way our lives currently are and how a current situation is working out, things will start to change.

Law of Sustenance – That which emerges from the complexities of natural processes.

Law of Sympathetic Magic – The belief that what one does to a physical object, which belonged to a person, or to a representation of the person, will similarly affect that person. This law is based upon the Law of Similarity and the Law of Contagion or Contact.

442 Cosmic & Universal Laws
Dottie Randazzo

Law of Sympathetic Resonance – Sound is used to identify and correct imbalances on all levels of being.

Law of Sympathy – An assumption that mental and historical associations retain real world material influences. This law "resolves" itself into two more specific laws, the Law of Similarity and the Law of Contiguity.

Law of Synchronicity – Being in the perfect place at the perfect time. Also known as the Law of Grace.

Law of Synthesis – The synthesis of two opposing or conflicting, ideas or pieces of data will produce a new, third idea that will not be a compromise of the original two. *See also Law of Opposites and Law of Polarity.*

442 Cosmic & Universal Laws
Dottie Randazzo

Law of Tao – Time is a screen upon which all things are projected. All movements upon that screen are movements in the here and now.

Law of Teaching – The responsibility people have to pass on that which they learn, for the continuation of the human race to benefit by this information.

Law of Telepathy – Governs communication between minds by some means other than sensory perception.

Law of Tenfold – Universal principle wherein gifts freely given for spiritual use return to the grantor good fortune in equal to or greater than ten times the loss.

Law of Thermo-Dynamics – A body of higher heat or energy can transfer heat or energy to a body of lower heat or energy, but the lower body of heat or energy cannot transfer heat or energy to the higher body of heat or energy unless the lower body exerts enough energy to do so.

Law of Thinking – As a man thinketh, so he is.

Law of Thought – Energy follows thought; those who wish to energize, need only to direct their thoughts toward that target which needs energizing.

Law of Threefold Return – Anything you send out into the universe will return to you threefold. *See also Law of Cause & Effect, Law of Creativity and Law of Compensation.*

Law of Three Requests – Whenever we pray or request a higher power to assist, we bring stronger energy to the effort by repeating our request/prayer three times.

Law of Time – The only moment we have is now. This is where we create.

Law of Time Preference – One always prefers earlier rather than later in satisfaction of a desire.

Law of Tithing – This cosmic law is usually applied for prosperity; however, it is not restricted to such. The vital attitude behind this law is that of sincerity. The law works truly if we give in all sincerity without expecting anything in return.

Law of Tolerance – That which recognizes the divinity in others, even when covered by their masks and armor of demonic imagery and activities or hidden behind the walls of apparent ignorance, sleep and stupidity, inspires us to recognize the divinity in all. *See also Law of Respect.*

Law of Transmissive Vibraic Energy – All forms of transmissive energy can be focused, reflected, refracted, transformed and diminished in intensity inversely as the square distance from the original source.

Law of Transmutation – Man has the privilege of transmuting his environment, reality and being into something more glorious.

Law of the Triangle – The three points of the triangle are responsible for the manifestation of all things in the finite plane. *See also Law of Trinity.*

442 Cosmic & Universal Laws
Dottie Randazzo

Law of Trinity – Symbolizes the triune functions and qualities of all creative energies in the universe. These energies give birth to the Law of Formation, sustains the Law of Preservation and transforms the Law of Disintegration, all manifestations, phenomena, conditions, circumstances and all experiences. Also known as the Law of the Triangle.

Law of Triple Invocation – All invocations must occur three times to be successful.

Law of True Falsehoods – If it's a paradox, the paradox is probably true. *See also Law of Infinite Universes and Law of Pragmatism.*

Law of Uncertainty – Life does not guarantee anyone anything. Nothing is certain in a relativistic sense. Everything has an unknown side or counterpart. *See also Law of Probability and Law of Averages.*

Law of Unconditional Love – Loving ourselves and other people as they are honoring self and another's self and soul path.

Law of Unforeseen Consequences – Any purposeful action will produce some unforeseen consequences. *See also Law of Unintended Consequences.*

Law of Unintended Consequences – Any purposeful action will produce some unintended consequences. Also known as Law of Unforeseen Consequences.

Law of Unity – That which recognizes no separateness which ignores the appearance and seemingness of separateness in the apparent divisions of polarities, gender, cause and effects, the part and the whole, the one and the many: but realizing these each as integrated parts of the total picture. *See also Law of Chance, Law of Gratitude and Law of Magic.*

Law of Unity & Diversity – For unity diversity must be honored.

Law of Universal Influence – You can never take anything for granted, no matter how small or insignificant it may seem.

Universal Law – Knowledge that awareness of all living things, all life, has within it the vitality and strength to gather from itself all things necessary for its growth and fruition.

442 Cosmic & Universal Laws
Dottie Randazzo

Law of Universal Sympathy – Allows a person who is devoid of the ego principal to transfer information or influence another's mind.

Law of The Universe – You have earned the gifts that you have. You evolve by using the gifts that you have earned. If you want to experience the miraculous then you must devote your energies, time and lives toward this goal.

Law of Vacuum – Energies create a vacuum behind them. This vacuum draws forth other energies. When individuals move toward higher levels of consciousness, these individuals create a vacuum, which draws others to fill that void which, the individual left behind.

Law of Values – What we truly value and believe in is reflected in our actions, even though our words may say otherwise.

Law of Variability – Anything true is variable. The world has changed or transformed and will continue to change on the basis of this law. *See also Law of Changeability.*

Law of Vibration – Any vibration which is sent out for good or service, increases into higher frequencies as it moves through space until it returns to its origin, bringing the gifts of those higher frequencies.

Law of Visualization – You must see it in your mind before you can achieve it. This law works in conjunction with the Law of Attraction. *See also Law of Affinity, Law of Pure Desire, Law of Paradoxical*

Intent, Law of Magnetism, Law of Coalesce, Law of Harmony and Law of Imaging.

Law of Will of God – It is God's will that what is human should be divine, and therefore all creation pushes forth to the God light.

Law of Will of Power – Is the individual drive within a soul extension/personality, which is projected, from the complete entity.

Law of Wisdom – If you have the wisdom to learn your lessons through love and wisdom you can mitigate your suffering. Wisdom erases karma.

Law of Words of Power – Refers to terms like teacher, professor, doctor, technician, and priest. *See also Law of Names.*

Law of World View Perspective – Our conception, interpretations and beliefs concerning outer reality plays a definite role in determining the reality that we experience.

Printed in Great Britain
by Amazon